THY KINGDOM COME

Thy Kingdom Come
By
Jonah Awodeyi

ISBN 978-1-4466-6728-6

Sponsored and printed by New Life Teaching Ministry

Published by Lulu.com

Printed in Great Britain.

Acknowledgment

Thanks be to God who had enabled us write this little book. We hope and prayed that its message of spiritual encouragement and challenges would be a blessing to all that read it. May I also thank all my family and friends who have encouraged me by giving their time and support. My two daughters, Dorcas and Elizabeth, who have contributed and helped in the editing of the book, and my son, Enoch who has supported us financially. I sincerely thank Rev. Amos Komolafe, my brother in law, for his endless contribution and support. May I also appreciate my Christian friend, Ngozi Onbuya, for her friendship, support and contributions. Thanks to Kunle Ibironke, who gave immense support and printing insight to the printing of the book. Thanks to Pastor John whose contribution to the first chapter has inspired the writing of the remaining chapters. May God richly bless you all. My greatest gratitude goes to my wife Lydia who had endured and sacrificed a lot – 'A good wife who can find'.

Contents

Preface

This little book is a collection of a few Christian tracts that I wrote to remind us (Christians) that the work of the kingdom is not over. The inspiration came with the revelation that 'the Lord's prayer' is not just a disciple's prayer, or a prayer to be analysed and patterned after, but it is the very heart of Jesus Christ. It is the total package of the mission of Jesus on planet earth: and how He perceived His mission.

The church must catch this vision, focus on it, and live by it. Failure to grasp this, means failure in any other thing we do. God's priority is to regain the dominion and power over mankind's world, which was freely handed to Satan, and enable mankind to be obedient once again. Therefore, 'the Lord's prayer' must daily be renewed and refreshed in our minds, with our eyes focused on every word in it. May He in His mercy strengthen our hearts with the words of His vision –'Thy will be done on earth as it is done in heaven'. Amen

CHAPTER 1

THE KINGDOM CALL

"My kingdom is not of this world" John 18:36

I felt the compulsion in my spirit to sound this waking call to all God's children who have been born again by the Spirit of the Lord. We seem to have forgotten our holy calling into the kingdom of God, pursuing instead our daily bread and pleasure of the world. Hence, we take very lightly the prayer of the Lord Jesus Christ, which He taught the first disciples –
"Our Father who art in heaven, Hallowed be thy name, Thy kingdom come, Thy will be done on earth as it is in heaven" (Mathew 6:9,10).

When I became born again and was growing up we were taught that this prayer is irrelevant for us since we now know how to pray through the Holy Spirit. We also learnt that the Lord had used this prayer, as a pattern or guide to enable the disciples to pray but the disciples did not follow this pattern after they received the Holy Spirit.

Of course, it was a teaching and a pattern that was never mentioned in the epistles, but we do not know the effectiveness of this prayer in their lives and especially in the life of Jesus, the great teacher. If it was important to Jesus to teach this 'kingdom prayer' we must sincerely take it beyond a "patterned prayer" and seriously begin to consider it as essential to the kingdom of God's message, which we preach.

The kingdom prayer is the foundation and the batch of the gospel messages. It is the embodiment of the preaching of Jesus and the apostles and must not be taken lightly. It is the main reason why Jesus was sent into the world. To us, the sacrificial death is extremely important, but to God the establishment of His reign and dominion on earth, as well as regaining man's obedience is paramount. Hence, Jesus focused His preaching and teachings on the kingdom of heaven and its King, God the Father.

According to His statement in John 17:6, another of His prayers, which reads *'I manifested thy name to the men whom Thou gavest Me out of the world'* we begin to understand the high priority Jesus gave to the knowledge of God and the doing of His will (obedience) as the angels do in heaven. Why should God take the pain to forgive us if the highest priority is not establishing His authority in man's world and enabling man to be obedient to His sovereign rule? God loved man from the beginning of time so much so that He was prepared to give His Son as a sacrifice for his (man's) sin thereby delivering man from his enemy, Satan.

However, the first relationship, grounded in obedience, trust, and respect must be restored so that man can resume fellowship with his Creator: whom Jesus now presents as the heavenly Father, worshipped and revered by the heavenly beings. Just as forgiveness is empty without sacrifice so is fellowship empty without obedience. This is the essential ingredient in this kingdom prayer.

Jesus did not intend it merely as a pattern for prayer, though we call it the Lord's Prayer, but that His disciples should make it their own prayer. Neither is it a mere teaching that we should overlook. Instead, it is a serious godly conviction to meditate, contemplate, practice, and constantly refresh in our minds. By doing this, we remind ourselves of the purpose of our salvation; which is to see the kingdom of God established in our world again.

Constant praying in this manner *'thy kingdom come'* is a courteous request from us to our heavenly Father that we desire His rule and the authority in our lives and in our world. It also indicates that we are rejecting the present spiritual rulers and authorities influencing our world and the lives of our loved ones. In addition, our request demonstrates to Satan and the spiritual world that we have chosen, voluntarily, to have the angelic lifestyle, obedience to the Father. Above all it shows our willingness to do God's will now on earth, and our gratitude to God the Father who loved us whilst we were still His enemies.

When God opened my eyes to this kingdom prayer I was ashamed to be called a child of God, because I found that the kingdom prayer came with a kingdom lifestyle.

Of course I'm born into His kingdom by the grace of God, however, I found that, unlike the Angels in heaven, I am not living the kingdom lifestyle whole-heartedly. Though I claimed to live in the kingdom of God I found that my standard of living was not that of the kingdom of heaven by far. I found it a big struggle to yield myself to doing His will, as demonstrated by the life of Jesus during His earthly ministry.

Many times we have chosen the easy path, allowing our common sense to override the will of God, which is the toughest choice. We forget the words of Jesus that state the way to abundant life is narrow. We also forget that it was common sense that got Adam into trouble (disobedience). Hence, we read in 2 Corinthians 10:4-6 that 'common sense' is the strong hold of disobedience to the will of God

"For the weapons of our warfare are not of the flesh, but divinely powerful for the destruction of fortresses. We are destroying speculations and every lofty thing raised up against the knowledge of God, and we are taking every thought captive to the obedience of Christ, and we are ready to punish all disobedience, whenever your obedience is complete".

2 Corinthians 10:5,6 gives us a break down of the warfare against the nature of our common sense that were fortresses –

1. Speculation
2. Knowledge

3. Thoughts
4. Disobedience

I was previously of the opinion that commonsense had nothing to do with Christian living until I realised the power of commonsense was overtaking my will to obey God. The predominant assumption is that we had the mind of Christ when we became believers. This is true as far as God is concerned, but untrue humanly speaking because the passage in Romans 12:2 calls for the transformation of the mind, which demands our considerations. It reads –

"And do not be conformed to this world, but be transformed by the renewal of your mind, that you may prove what the will of God is, that which is good and acceptable and perfect".

It is a well-known fact that we all came to Christ just as we are: not only with our baggage of sins but also with a polluted and corrupted mind that was in total control of our lives (*"you were formerly alienated and hostile in mind, engaged in evil deeds" Colossians 1:21).* Our minds then become the battlefield for the warfare between our will and the will of God, between commonsense and faith. Hence we find ourselves struggling to trust God in some instances because commonsense dictates otherwise.

It would be misleading to assume that I am stating that our commonsense is of no value. No, for the passage (2 Corinthians 10:5,6) clearly indicates that commonsense must be taken captive to the obedience of Christ, and our knowledge yielded to the knowledge of God.

Moreover, Proverb 3:5,6 clearly states we must not rely on our own understanding because it may not yield a perfect result according to the purpose and plan of God for us, but instead we must acknowledge (surrender to) God in all our ways –

"Trust in the Lord with all your heart, and do not lean on your own understanding. In all your ways acknowledge Him, and He will make your paths straight" Proverb 3:5,6.

It is this ability to completely trust the Lord with all our hearts, in all lives' endeavour, that is frequently under attack by our commonsense. 'Why should I trust God in this little situation that I can easily resolve' becomes the mind's question. Another thought that comes our way is that 'if God did not want me to use my brain He won't have given it to me in the first place, would He?'

In response these mental attacks, James tells us that there are two types of wisdom – earthly wisdom and heavenly wisdom. For we read in James 3:13-15 these words –

"Who amongst you is wise and understanding? Let him show me his good behaviour his deeds in the gentleness of wisdom. But if you have bitter jealousy and selfish ambition in your heart, do not be arrogant and so lie against the truth. This

wisdom is not that which comes down from above, but is earthly, natural and demonic".

We know that heavenly wisdom comes from God and that it is only given to them who obey Him. Therefore we must make every effort to bring our commonsense captive to the obedience of Christ so that we may obtain pure wisdom from above.

When obedience is restored into our lives, and the determinations to doing God's will is upheld, then God's ways become our ways and pure wisdom is revealed. Then, we begin to grow in the mind of Christ, which has obedience as its foundation, and we shall be able to say to God our Father 'I exist to do Your will' just as Jesus did saying *'I have come to do* Your will'. Our confession, coupled with our daily prayer 'Thy kingdom come' will stimulate an angelic lifestyle within our hearts and enable us to focus on His kingdom reign on planet earth.

May Righteousness, Peace, and Joy in the Holy Spirit be with you (Romans 14:17). Amen.

CHAPTER 2

THE KINGDOM'S CITY

"You have come to mount Zion and the city of the living God" Hebrews 12:22

I suppose the biggest question confronting every Christian is 'what is the kingdom of God?' as presented by Jesus and preached by the disciples. The Lord Jesus Christ in His prayer instructed His disciples to focus on this one thing when they pray 'thy kingdom come': whilst He taught in many words and parables what the kingdom of God is about.

The recorded parables clearly teach that the kingdom of God is precious, costly, homely, and rewarding (Matthews 13). It cannot be compared with the finest commodity on earth therefore man must search for it and be prepared to sell all their possession in order to purchase it and make it theirs. Nevertheless it is a city without foundation or walls, which everyone on planet earth should aspire to enter.

According to scripture godly men and women of old desired this city so much that they were ready to sacrifice everything for it but they were denied because the gates were not yet opened for all mankind to come in *("All these died in faith, without receiving the promises, but having seen them and having welcomed them from a distance, and having confessed that they were strangers and exiles on the earth...they desired a better country, that is a heavenly one" Hebrews 11:13-16).*

Therefore they were satisfied to constrict their aspirations for the city to being strangers and aliens on earth until the gates are opened. With the arrival, death, and resurrection of Jesus, and His blood made available for man's sin, the keys to the kingdom was released and given to man. According to the scripture that reads, *"I will give you the keys of the kingdom of heaven" (Matthew 16:19),* access was granted, and the city's assets was made available for all who find it. God released His blessings to earthly citizens according to the passage that reads, "Blessed be the God and Father of our Lord Jesus Christ, who has blessed us with every spiritual blessing in the heavenly places in Christ" Ephesians 1:3. These keys, therefore, are meant to unlock both the earthly city and the heavenly city gates. "Whatever you bind on earth shall be bound in heaven, and whatever you shall loose on earth shall be loosed in heaven," said Jesus (Matthews 16:19). This affirms the teachings of the 'Lord's Prayer, "Thy will be done on earth as it is in heaven"; and firmly placed the kingdom of God on planet earth. Paul also spoke about God bringing him safely to His heavenly kingdom in 2 Timothy 4:18 to indicate the transition from the earthly kingdom.

Therefore, from the teachings of our Lord Jesus Christ in the gospel of John 3:3,6, which reads "truly, truly, I say to you unless one is born again, he cannot see the kingdom of God": and "truly, truly, I say to you unless one is born of water and the Spirit, he cannot enter into the kingdom of God", we gained the understanding that the kingdom of God is not only a distant event but also that of the present. According to Jesus, the will of God must be done now on earth as the angels do in heaven. Talking to the religious leaders of His days regarding the where about of the kingdom of God, Jesus also pointed out that 'the kingdom of God is in your midst' and there is no specific location for it (Luke 17:20,21).

Since this is the case, the location of the kingdom city depends entirely on its king, Jesus. It also becomes clear that there are some who will see the city, and those who will strive hard to enter into it. Seeing and entering the city begins from the very moment the decision is made to follow Jesus. Nevertheless there are two groups of followers: those that will see the kingdom of God (the kingdom city) now, and enjoy the wealth: and those that strive hard to enter the city and become its citizen by embracing its lifestyle.

The first group are satisfied followers who have found the city because they have been born again according to John 3:3. And they enjoy the fringe benefits of the kingdom because they have been translated from the kingdom of darkness into the kingdom of light. But they are neither in nor out. They bounce in and out of the kingdom like a tennis ball played on a tennis court, whenever they feel like because they live on the edge of the kingdom. They are not ready to follow Jesus into the city in order settle down and live its lifestyle.

A comparison is seen in the redemption account of the children of Israel from Egypt during the days and leadership of Moses. When they miraculously crossed the Red Sea, and saw their enemies destroyed, they celebrated jubilantly with songs and dancing. But they soon forgot the purpose of their deliverance, which was to fellowship and have personal relationship with their God. Instead their minds were constantly longing for the little enjoyment they had as slaves in the land of Egypt. Food, drink, and pleasure became their desires. Once, they elected a leader to lead them back to the land of slavery as they despised angelic food that God provided for the journey. They did not fully understand the purpose of their election and deliverance. Therefore God was 'wounded to the heart' that He decided none of them would enter the Promised Land: because they lack the knowledge of God despite testing God ten times regarding provisions.

The same gratitude is seen with this first group as they demonstrate contentment with the so called 'prosperity messages', but despised messages that will change their life-style and challenge their relationship with God. Their only interest and relationship in God is based on the blessings or riches they have or do not have. Though Jesus clearly warned that a person's life is not measured by the abundance of things he or she has

(Luke 12:15), their ears are readily in-tune with passages of scriptures that point to the wealth of the city. For this group of Christians Jesus' teaching and encouragement to the citizen of the kingdom to ask whatever is needed, is purely rooted in financial gain. They failed to see that this encouragement is for those who have sold all they possessed to make the city theirs just as in the parable of the hidden treasure in Matthew 13:14. This man in the parable found the treasure, hid it, sold all that he has, and bought the entire field in order to settle there. Perhaps members of this first group would have taken the treasure away with them rather than live on the field. For these the amount of money in their bank accounts and protection received measures spirituality. May God be merciful on such Christians.

But the second group will not settle for the crumbs of the land. They are determined to settle in the city, gain citizenship, and live its lifestyle. According to Jesus' statement in John 3:6 about seeing and entering into the kingdom, they did not only see it to enjoy its fringe benefits, they were prepared to enter into the kingdom of God and settle down. They would rather take hold of its richest blessing and assets, which are the knowledge of God and building relationship with the King, than to merely obtain provisions and protections. For such Christians the lifestyle of the city is precious than its material blessings, because they know that the kingdom of God is not food and drink (provision of daily needs and the pleasure of living) but Righteousness, Peace, and Joy in the Holy Spirit (Romans 14:17).

Their standard of living is the desire to know God better and better, thereby improving their relationship with Him according to Paul's prayers for the Ephesians' Christians (Ephesians 1:15-19). This is paramount and not negotiable with material gains, that is anything, when compared with the deepest knowledge of walking with God in holiness and righteousness. They are people ever ready to declare with the prophet Habakkuk the statement of faith –

"Though the fig tree should not blossom, and there be no fruit on the vines, though the yield of the olive should fail, and the fields produce no food, though the flock should be cut off from the flock and there be no cattle in the stalls, yet I will exult in the Lord, I will rejoice in the God of my salvation" (3:17,18).

These would not settle for life alone but hunger and thirst for the abundant life, which Jesus promised to give – *'I came that they might have life and might have it abundantly'* (John 10:10). Again this abundant life has nothing to do with financial gain. It is simply a tranquillity of the mind, which life situations cannot disturb. It may be shaken like a strong wind blows on a tree and shakes its branches and leaves, but its roots are deep in the soil. For these Christians their 'stomach is not their god' according to Paul's observation of some Christian in Philippi (Philippians 3:19), and their God is not exchangeable for provisions. They have a different spirit like Joshua and Caleb in the days of Moses, and want the city and its lifestyle at all cost; neither will they settle for anything less. Are you one of these?

"And the street of the city was pure gold, like transparent glass. And I saw no temple in it, for the Lord God, the Almighty, and the Lamb, are its temple. And the city has no need of sun or of moon to shine upon it, for the glory of God has illumines it, and its lamp is the Lamb" Revelation 21:21-23.

CHAPTER 3

THE KINGDOM'S ENEMY

"Your enemy, the devil, prowls about like a roaring lion" 1 Peter 5:8

The worst crime a military tactician may commit during a time of war is to underestimate the strength of the enemy's army. We have seen battles won and lost due to the tactic deployed by the military brain. History has recorded battles that were lost because the strength of the enemy was belittled. In such cases the enemy won the challenge and embarrassed the might of its opponent. This was the situation in the campaign of Joshua against a little city called Ai (Joshua 7,8). Joshua had seen the mighty defence of the city of Jericho crumble and crippled by his army. He had also secured remarkable victories over mighty Kings and warriors. In fact the name Joshua and his God became the fear of the surrounding neighbours causing them to surrender and make peace. But on one occasion, his tacticians miscalculated the strength of this small city and thereby suggested that Joshua should not attack the city in full strength. The outcome was embarrassing, as Joshua's army was defeated. Realising his mistake, he consulted God for the best manoeuvres to deploy against the city. God showed him what to do for his second attempt. With such a brilliant mind and strategy he became victorious. It is clear therefore that he won because of the strategy deployed not by the strength of his army.

King David had similar experience when he fled for his life due to the rebellion of his son Absalom. He knew his greatest military tactician and adviser (Ahithophel) had teamed up with his rebel son and whatever plans this man marked out would be successful (2 Samuel 16:20-23). Ahithophel was the most feared and respected person in the land during times of war. Any suggestion given by him was mightier than swords. And should Absalom embarked on his tactful suggestions David will be a fugitive for a very long time, forever running for his life. So he (David) prayed against the counsel of this one man saying -

"O Lord, I pray, make the counsel of Ahithophel foolishness" (2 Samuel 15:31).

God heard his prayers and defused this man's tact to attack David immediately while he was weak and tired. Absalom rejected his plan, and Ahithophel killed himself -

"Now when Ahithophel saw that his counsel was not followed.... (he) set his house in order, and strangled himself" 2 Samuel 17:23.

A similar thing happens daily in our Christian lives when we underestimate the strength of the small things such as "white lies" here and there, bending the truth slightly in our favour, or a one off cheat that we promised would be the last one. Sometimes, if not often, it is that small job that we take for granted that demands much of our time and energy. This also is spiritually true when we overlook the tactics our enemy (Satan) deploys in small doses. We know that Satan himself is limited, and can only be at one place at a given time, yet when he operates no man or angels can stop him. The only One that will put an end to him is God, according to Romans 16:20 (*"And the God of peace will soon crush Satan under your feet"*).
Paul found this a recordable experience in his letter to the Thessalonians when he wrote

'For we wanted to come to you--I, Paul, more than once--and yet Satan thwarted (obstructed) us' (1 Thessalonians 2:18).

Michael, the commander of the heavenly host of angels found that he was no match for Satan when he came to claim the body of Moses according to Jude 9, which reads –

"But Michael the archangels, when he disputed with the devil and argued about the body of Moses, did not dare pronounce against him a railing judgment but said 'the lord rebuke you'".

He, Satan is a brilliant tactician. He is nothing like the caricature portray we have of him with horns on his head and a fork in his deadly hands. Far be it from the truth.

The biblical portrayal of him is found in Ezekiel 28:11- 19 which contains statements such as 'you had the seal of perfection, full of wisdom and perfect in beauty', 'every precious stone was your covering', and 'you were the anointed cherub who covers'. In actual fact, Satan was formally one of the Seraphim that stood in the presence of God covered with their wings (Isaiah 6:1-4).

He reads and quotes from the bible and carries it about all the time (Matthew 4:6). James said he trembles and deeply reverend God (James 2:19). Paul informs us that he is crafty, witty, canny, and a great fighter according to Ephesians 6:11-

"Put on the full armour of God that you may be able to stand against the schemes (wiles, plots, devices) of the devil".

We also know that he sometimes changes to become an angel of light (2 Corinthians 11:14) in order to deceive us, pretending to be our friend just like he did with Adam and Eve in the garden. But Jesus warns us about him saying he is a thief, murderer, destroyer, liar, and the father of lies. For these reasons the bible presents him as 'a roaring lion looking for someone to devour' 1 Peter 5:8.

In order to understand this warning from Peter we must understand the tactics of the lioness as she attacks her prey. She moves cunningly, softly and slowly, with an intense look and full concentration, weighing out the strengths and weaknesses of her prey. After identifying her target, be it the strayed away, the weaklings, or the young without adults' protection, she pounces swiftly in fast movements, to attack and kill her target.

Sometimes I feel like screaming when I hear some Christians say 'Satan is a lion without teeth'. Such statement is bad strategy and belittles our ferocious enemy. We underestimate Satan at our peril for he has teeth and will use it for the kill. This is why Peter said 'be alert', or 'be on the lookout'. If we are caught sleeping with our defences down, he will not spare his prey. He will chew it to the bones.

He laughs at us when we fail to see him as a dangerous enemy who will stop at nothing to find and devour his victim. He is a killing machine just as Jesus pointed out. We may banish him as many times as we can, pull down as many of his stronghold as possible, yet he never gives up waiting for an opportunity to pounce. His banner reads 'you can't keep me down'. To forge a peace treaty with him is a waste of time and effort for he definitely will not keep his side of the truce. Jesus said 'he is a liar and his native language is lies'. There is no truth in him. Neither can we be completely free of him in this lifetime nor wave him away with the power God invested in us, since he is nicked name 'the accuser of the brethren'.

On the contrary, the Holy Spirit warns us to be vigilant, watchful, stand in the full armour of God, and hold firmly our shields so that we might be able to wade off all the flaming missiles of the evil one (Satan) Ephesians 6:13-17. Satan is poised to attack at any given opportunity: and we must be aware of this

"In order that no advantage be taken of us by Satan; for we are not ignorant of his schemes" 2 Corinthians 2:11.

Therefore we must listen to the clear warnings of the Holy Spirit, who will not belittle the strength and tactics of this known adversary. The writer of Hebrews emphasised that 'we are surrounded by great could of witnesses (Christians who have successfully fought this enemy), watching and saying to us "Fix your eyes on Jesus, the Author and Perfecter of Faith. Do not give the enemy any openings by holding on to unnecessary weight (life burden) and sin that clings on too easily"' Hebrews 12:1- 5. The enemy is poised, weighing us out; so we must be watchful, alert, and pray for more strength'.

Lastly in the prayer recorded in John 17 Jesus prayed for all His followers saying to the Father "I do not ask Thee to take them out of the world, but to keep them from the evil one" thereby expressing His concern for us, knowing that we shall be ferociously attack by Satan when He is gone.

Christian Friend WATCHOUT.

1 *CHRISTIAN, seek not yet repose,*
Cast thy dreams of ease away;
Thou art in the midst of foes:
Watch and pray.

2 *In the heavenlies see that land,*
Satan would thine entrance stay;
Thou against his wiles must stand:
Watch and pray.

3 *Principalities and powers,*
Mustering their unseen array,
Wait for thy unguarded hours:
Watch and pray.

4 *Gird thy heavenly armour on,*
Wear it ever, night and day;
Ambushed lies the evil one:
Watch and pray.

5 *Hear the victors who o'er came;*
Still they mark each warrior's way;
All with one sweet voice exclaim:
Watch and Pray

By Charlotte Elliott (1789 – 1871)

CHAPTER 4

JESUS IS COMING! ARE YOU READY?

"Just as it happened in the days of Noah" (Luke 17:26)

It is common knowledge and practice by everybody to get ready for any journey before the departure date in order not to miss the scheduled time. If going in a car, one ensures that the car has enough petrol for the journey, water in the carburettor and the tyres are inflated to the required sizes. Clothes are washed and packed. And all other items for the journey are considered. If we have to pick up a friend on our way, this friend must also be well prepared in advance and ready to be picked up. If it was to catch a flight we endeavour to be at the airport some hours before the time the plane takes off. Failure to check in at least 30 minutes before take off will result in us missing that flight.

This same principle applies to the warning given by Jesus that we must 'be ready' so that we may not miss Him when He comes again the second time. Matthew 24:42 –44 reads

"Therefore be on the alert, for you do not know which day your Lord is coming. But be sure of this that if the head of house had known at what time of the night the thief was coming, he would have been on the alert and would not have allowed his house to be broken into. For this reason you be ready too, for the Son of man is coming at an hour when you do not think He will".

This warning is incredibly difficult and serious since there is no arranged time, and no pick up spot! Imagine you have been longing to go to a beautiful island with your best friend who has convinced you to come with him. But unfortunately he did not tell you when you will both leave for this island. No date or time was given. Neither did he tell you he had or was going to book the flight or arrange transportation for this blessed journey. But all he was able to say to you is 'hi guys! I'm not sure when the journey is taking place but make sure you are always ready to leave whenever I call to pick you up. Get your bags packed for I can drop in any day and at any time'. Not many friends will accept this as a genuine invitation. Perhaps only a handful that believe in their friendship and trust their friend will endeavour to get ready and anticipate their best friend serious proposition.

But the Lord Jesus went much more further to help His friends so that they might be ready by giving them the signs to look out for with regard to His coming. We read in Luke 21:34,36

"Be on your guard that your hearts may not be weighed down with dissipation and drunkenness and worries of life and that day come on you suddenly like a trap, for it will come upon all those who dwell on the face of all the earth. But keep alert at all times".

Please note these three things that mark the closeness of His coming timetable and relate them to today's society

1. Dissipation (unrestrained indulgence in physical pleasures)

2. Drunkenness (party spirit, play time, and pleasure)

3. Worries of life (daily bread and clothing).

How close are we to the Lord's coming one wonder? We read in Luke 17:26- 28 that,

"Just as it happened in the days of Noah, so it shall be also in the days of the Son of Man... it was the same in the days of Lot".

Society will have similar social life as the people in Noah's (approximately 3000 BC) and Lot's (approximately 2000 BC) days. These group of people experienced divine visitation and judgement during those days because they were not anticipating it. As far as they were concerned life went on as usual. They were into serious partying, business, pleasure, living and food costing, and resolving accommodation problems. While the then world was completely focused on pleasure and rebuilding, social morality was declining and sinking into its graveyard.

Our society is even worst compared to these two groups of societies. We have added 'godlessness, lovers of self and money, haters of good, and brutality' to our list as predicted over 2000 years ago (2 Timothy 3:1-5). It is sad to see the society firmly engaged with social pleasures and little or no time for the coming of Jesus. The world of mankind was fast asleep spiritually and physically the first time He came. Only few devout men and women were on the lookout for His coming though it was prophesied many years earlier. This time we must not be caught napping. As His followers we must be ready, packed, and have our backs turned to the pleasures this world have to offer; for whosoever love the world and its pleasures, does not have the love of God in him or her. Neither must we be tired of waiting nor let our lamps burn out because He will come suddenly and without warning.

Christian friend, check it out; our time is up. The Master is on His way and will arrive sooner then we think. Are you packed and ready?

"Therefore, be on the alert, for you do not know when the master of the house is coming, whether in the evening, at midnight, at cockcrowing, or in the morning, lest he come suddenly and find you asleep. What I say to you I say to all, 'Be on the alert'" Mark 11:35,36.

CHAPTER 5

THE KING'S RETURN

'When the Son of Man comes, will He find faith on the earth?' (Luke 18:8)

This is the million, million pound sterling question that demands an answer; and every generation has responded the best way they can since it was asked over 2000 years ago by the Master. Many have taken their stand, refusing to be deterred or defeated, knowing that the Lord Jesus Christ can come at any given time; while others have compromised their faith and took a tumble away from the straight and narrow way. 1 Timothy 1:19 reads "keeping faith and a good conscience, which some have rejected and suffered shipwreck in regard to their faith". Persecution and love for this present world's pleasure led to the down fall of many during their time on earth. For such, their faith only lasted for a while and faded away at the sight of difficulties and lust. Should the Master have come during their days He would have been disappointed.

When I became a born again Christian in the early seventies, this verse from Luke 18:8 became one of my strongholds. I considered it my responsibility to hold on to my faith regardless of whatever came my way. I strongly believed Jesus could come at any time for His disciples and I didn't want to miss 'the heavenly train'. My pastor did not make it easy for us as he constantly reminded us that persecution was part of our Christian package.

I clearly remember him saying 'if you are a Christian and have not experienced persecutions or insults from family and friends for His sake, you better examine your live, maybe you have not truly given your life to Jesus. Satan might still be pleased with your lifestyle and has not disowned you. So why don't you challenge Satan and tell him you no longer belong to his camp and await his reaction. He will certainly come to test you'. So it was with us in those days, challenging Satan to test our faith. If this common enemy of righteousness constantly tested Jesus' faith you and I will not be spared. As young Christians we only had one thing in our minds, which was to prepare for the return of the Master. There was no time for prosperity messages. It was about holding on to the cross and not letting go or giving up.

In addition we read books about Christians' persecution in places like Russia, the old communist block, and their stand for Jesus. One of the books contained a story of a Christian who gave up his tiny blanket to cover another Christian, as they both slept in the open field on a winter day. As they lay there, the one thought in this brother's mind as he watched the other brother shivering in the cold weather was 'if that was Christ would you give Him your blanket?' So he covered the brother with his own blanket. Would you have done the same for Jesus realising that meant your death?

Once or twice we were stoned by angry mobs during an open-air evangelism. Some still have the scars to show for it. Parents disowned some because of their faith, yet they joyfully declared that Jesus was the only way to Heaven. I remember the dad of one converted Muslim sister asked her what he should do to stop her from following Jesus. In response she said 'the only way to stop me is by operation; you will have to cut me open in halves in order to remove Jesus who lives inside of me'.

There were many testimonies of persecution and how the brethren stood for their faith. These, like the first apostles, would not be intimidated into compromising their faith. They were men and women like Peter, Paul, and John, to name a few, who waited for the coming of the Master, Jesus; and would not cave in under persecution. They ensured that their faith was kept alive, and were determined not to disappoint the Master when He comes. Their cry for the Master was 'the Spirit and the bride say, "Come", and let the one who hears say, "Come"' (Revelation 22:17).

The first disciples expected the imminent return of Jesus, and died in their expectation keeping the flame of faith burning. When Paul the Apostle realised that his time on earth was coming to an end, he wrote to

Timothy saying 'I have fought the fight, I have kept the faith' (2 Timothy 4:7). With a similar voice he encouraged Timothy, who represented the up-coming Christian generation, spurring him on to 'Fight the good fight of faith, and take hold of the eternal life to which you were called' (1 Timothy 6:12).

Should the Master return today would He be disappointed at what He sees or would He pat our backs for fighting the good fight of faith? Would we be able to look straight unto His eyes and say to Him 'Master I have kept the faith'? Would we hear His voice saying to us 'you trusted and faithful servant enter into my rest', or would we hear 'depart from me you workers of iniquity (sinful workers)'? (Matthews 7:23)

This is our time to keep faith's fire burning more than ever, in man's history. This is the hour to take our stand for God and Christ declaring like Joshua "as for me and my household we have chosen the Lord God Jehovah" (Joshua 24:15).

The question still remains to be answered by you and I, "When the Son of Man comes will He find faith on earth?" This is not the faith of going to church; but that of living out the teaching of the Master in our present generation, the kingdom lifestyle.

Are you dependable and trustworthy, ready to fight against sin and evil, Satan and his demonic angels? The Master is looking for those who are not pre-occupied with the affairs of everyday life, and this present world but those anticipating the new world to come (2 Timothy 2:3,4).

Are you ready to meet Him face to face? What is your answer to His question? We all must provide an individual response. We must fight the good fight of faith to which we were called. Are you standing firm for Jesus and His kingdom in the face of persecutions and insult, or do you compromise your faith? Paul's steadfast instruction to the Christians of his days was "stand firm with the belt of truth and breastplate of righteous living". It is the Father's desire to give you the kingdom. Keep fighting and don't loss heart for the King is coming soon. "Behold I come quickly" is the cry from heaven; "the Spirit and the Brides respond is "Come Lord Jesus". He will come like a thief in the night; so don't be caught lapping. He will come sooner than you expect. Be strong in the Lord and in the power of His might. Amen.

"Jesus, I my cross have taken
All to leave and follow Thee
Destitute, despised, forsaken
Thou from hence, my all shall be
Perish every fond ambition
All I've sought, and hoped and known
Yet how rich is my condition
God and heaven are still my own".

By H. F. Lyre

www.ingramcontent.com/pod-product-compliance
Ingram Content Group UK Ltd.
Pitfield, Milton Keynes, MK11 3LW, UK
UKHW020229250726
13967UKWH00001B/272

9 781446 667286